The Things of This World

The Things of This World

Poems by

Michael Blanchard

Cover design by Shay Culligan
Cover image by Suuuu on Unsplash

ISBN: 979-8-90146-807-4

Kelsay Books
502 South 1040 East, A-119
American Fork, Utah 84003
Kelsaybooks.com

The true reckoning
of this world
is the way we come
to know things twice:
in the wonder first
and then the remembering.

Acknowledgments

Sincere thanks to the editors of the following journals, where some of the poems in this collection first appeared:

The Broad River Review: "Kingfisher"

Cave Region Review: "Counting Crows at Caney Creek," "Birding in the Bend"

Cold Mountain Review: "We are beautiful only"

MockingHeart Review: "Plowing at Sunrise," "Inheritance"

Stone Poetry Quarterly: "The Theory of Everything"

Streetlight Magazine: "The Things of This World"

Thanks also to friends and fellow poets Michael Hettich and Claire Hamner Matturro for their generous comments on the back cover, more generous perhaps than what is deserved.

And to two other friends and fellow poets, Suzanne Underwood Rhodes and Michelle Stoll, for their reading of an early version of the manuscript which eventually became this book and for their ongoing encouragement.

Contents

The Things of This World

More than one has said it:
that love is of this world only

the world of a willow
reaching for a river

as the river
goes its way

and of a nuthatch
nesting in a beechwood tree

as light devolves
from day into night

The true reckoning
of this world

is the way we come
to know things twice

in the wonder first
and then the remembering

the bitterroot blossom
before it fades

and everything else we lose
but love anyway

One and the Same

It's like stepping out
into the world
from the shade
of the alder grove

and into the sun
with each step
on the path
down to the lake

where the east
light glimmers
like a thousand scales
of truth—or chance

and the only sound's
the desultory hum
of bees
about the buckthorns

a bee too sees
the world complexly:
with simple eyes
oriented to light

and compound ones
of a thousand lenses
that form a single image
from a thousand scales

of truth—or chance
among its buckthorns
between the alder shade
and the glimmering lake

The Kingfisher

Does the hummingbird think he himself
invented his crimson throat?
—Mary Oliver

For just this once
look no further
than what simply is:

the fact of a kingfisher
beside a lake
not the one diving
or the one that speared
a stickleback with lance-like bill
but this one perched
on low branch
of a sweetgum tree
not contemplating
how fearfully it was made

It alit at the center
of the world

first in a dream
or a dream of a dream
indistinct in morning mist
but now in apprehension
a necessary appurtenance of wonder

with slate-blue crest
and rufous band
brilliant in the sun
not fearing if it loves God enough
or God loves it at all

the simple fact of a kingfisher
sufficient not in doing
or having but in seeing

Ordinary Time

In grey February
no subject is too small
with its days
unduly apportioned
from the year
and lying

in the valley of bones
between nativity
and resurrection

You find a pen
in the parking lot
of a grocery store
and write a letter
to an old friend
chronicling the day

and note the chance
intersection with
an anonymous life

You find yourself distracted
by the sudden flutter
of a window curtain
in an upstairs room
as you look for
an envelope and stamp

and consider the shape
wind assumes when
it animates a space

You hear music
faint from another room
and pause to listen
for a melody first
then the words
itinerant through the house

and hear in them
another February day
cold and snowless as this

and know in ordinary time
there is no mercy or blessing
only the relentless law of returning

Distraction

Attention is drawn
for a time
from words on a page
in a book on the desk

they say the Greeks knew
of moments that interrupt
the everyday flow of time
and enter as a gift

Outside the window
a fleshy pear
just ripe
distracts with its fullness

across the road
three horses in pasture
one black two roan
beckon with nod and snort

closer to mind
four apples on the window ledge
tempt with scent
of another autumn come due

one might be swayed
to share those with
pasture neighbors
and still be apple sufficient

Back on the desk
"Epiphany" is the word
Greeks had in mind
so much is plain

as black and white
so much plainer than ripened pears
or horses at the pasture gate
or four apples so red and so delicious

Season's End

Just a minute ago
I walked down
from the house

just far enough
to be out of its
circle of light

from here I can
see my life
or as much of it

as I need to see—
a half-moon scaled
on lake surface

a copse of pines
beyond
the rise of breeze

suggesting
the first return
of redwings

in the morning
or maybe
the morning after

Hunger

You go to bed hungry
and dream of comrades
and of feasting on flesh
of straight-horned cattle
sacred as those
that once grazed on the
hillsides of Thrinacia

There is in dream
no blood of slaughter
no crackling of roasting fire
no scent of fresh herbs
for seasoning

You wake up
wiser to the meaning
of hunger
but famished still
for the beef
that feed on sweet grass
of this waking world

cool milk from the ripe barn
and two warm eggs
freshly laid
which you hold
against your cheeks

on this chilly morning
for a moment
as if in a dream

The Wild Boar

We do this in remembrance
of him and his savage spirit:
with Argentine malbec and home-brew
feast on roasted loin of wild boar—
made tender by rosemary
lemon juice and slow mesquite—
and with wild rice and dark gravy
apricot sauce and grilled asparagus

We come to this table first
from the tracking of ferals
in a dry Arkansas fall
through trespassed fields into dense brush—
a silent breath a stillness in the Springfield sight
a shot through the lung then the loud exhalation
like a car tire going flat all at once
a heart shot to be sure and all was done

We come to this table
also from the task
of dragging dead weight almost equal my own
back to the truck with double yoke
one harnessed to forelegs
and one to my shoulders
glistening the grass as we returned
with bright blood and black bristle

And we come to this table from taking pause
at all things on earth and in heaven
which fashioned with savage grace in me
the beast that hungers for succulent flesh
of wild things, the man that thirsts to kill them,
and the god condemned for all days to be bound
to a body and drag it through
the broad brush and dry season of mortality

Sailing to China

All water is one
this boys know
from an early age

why else would they
build rafts of bamboo
poles lashed with rope

and baling wire
and launch them
in the canal

behind the house
with certainty of floating
to Hurricane Creek

and to the Mississippi
and from there
to the gulf

then gulf to ocean
all the way
to China—

that way of wind
and water less laborious
than a hole

dug straight through
earth's core
to the other side

or the long route
of Marco Polo
along the Silk Road

Boys know too
that water follows
a path

of least resistance
so sailing would
be easy

going with the flow
and with the warm
welcome by villagers

on the coast of China
in Shanghai say
or Shantou

What boys do not know
is that trade winds
blow where they will

and currents often flow
counter to will
or conventional wisdom

leaving them no closer
to their end
only to the mystery

Still, if anyone
asks for me
tell them I have

gone down to the river
and the last time
you saw me

I was toting rope
and a load
of bamboo

We are beautiful only

We are beautiful only
while we have bodies.
After that we are some
other body's prayer
for the dearly departed
to rest in peace eternal

On this side of the divide
nothing is eternal.

We are lovely bones,
though, that embrace
as long as there is
flesh on them.
We are the flesh too
and the blood.

We are the red too
of a camellia before
it is snipped and floats
in a glass bowl of cool water.
We are the bowl too
and the water.

We are the sweet fragrance
of wisteria as long
as they bloom
along the boulevard
clean like light rain.
We are the boulevard too.

We are the song
of the last sparrow to roost
before night gives way
to fireflies and crickets.
We are the spruce tree too
and the night.

On this side of beauty
nothing is eternal.

To be at home in this world
is not to own it
but to float
while the red still lasts
like camellias
in a bowl of cool bliss.

The Beginning of All Things

The night he died
was the last of the year—
our father, who is
in heaven I hope,
waited in death
as in life to see things
through until the end
settle the book
on all accounts
then close the cover

and leave survivors
to open our own book

written in a language
foreign as forgiveness
and needing translation
into the vernacular
of trespass and deliverance
to tell a story that begins
where all stories start
with the word *Once*
traced in dust
and then no more

After Snow

Dogwoods surprise first with white
before the pink
and the return of spring

as if to mock in their profusion
fierce snow now thawed
to a dissolute dew

or mimic in white
the March moon
pregnant with light

or lament the absence:
you have traveled over the mountain
and have not returned

in the space between
remains the chill and the low moon
nesting in dogwood branches

Slow Burn

Late in summer
the sun in the distant sky
roseate and warm
in its decline
is a sign
that the season too
will soon burn itself out
to an autumn ember

the kind of fire
that dies so slowly
we do not understand it
as dying or refining
but as a vague vulnerability
primal as fear

like waking up with you
in the same tent
cocooned in our separate bags
crawling out in the damp morning
to cold coffee and campfire ashes
and knowing we were
no longer the flame
and could never be the phoenix

Plowing at Sunrise

Something in morning air carries it
this rich acrid odor of decay:
compost and manure from fallow months
turned over onto themselves
and into furrows as day begins
moist still from
the last remembrance of night
and pale before the moon
fully concedes its place

Every year I return to this plot
denser soil muddies these boots
and each year tills
the leaves and squander of days
turns them over onto themselves
into a rich acrid field of now
moist with remembrance
pale and blind to color
until the sun rises red over the mountain

The House of Forgetting

In this house
that no longer stands
at the end of the street
that leads to nowhere

other than its amnesiac salons
with walls papered
in lilacs and cockatiels
where we converse over tea

while recollections of wrongs
percolate like French coffee
aromatic and dark
in propitiate kitchens

over oolong with lemon
my shadow brother
we make furtive alliance
with Time's redundancies

to lease them
basement rooms for cheap
on condition they are left
unperturbed

down where neither memory
nor hope nor regret
can defend us from dreams

in this house
that no longer stands
at the end of the street

The Day Elvis Died

this was
Icarus drowning
—William Carlos Williams

About 3:30 in the South
Tuesday mid-August

hot and dusty in the panhandle
between Dumas and Dalhart

family of three passing through
on the way to Colorado

father behind the wheel
of a two-toned Impala

they'll hear the news that night
and the weather report

at a motel in Pueblo
and eat burgers

over reruns
of *Happy Days* and *M*A*S*H*

meanwhile to the west
the nation tests a weapon

in nuclear Nevada
back-to-school sales

entice mothers
at Penny's and Sears

the Cardinals drop one
to the Mets five to one

and down the river in Memphis
where they found a fellow lifeless

on his bathroom floor
another little baby child

is born
at Baptist Memorial

Counting Crows at Caney Creek

If memory is a patch of earth
we walk over
and over again
this one is a stand
of bare trees in the preserve
late autumn
before the real cold descends.

A murder of crows congregates
on the skeletons of white oaks
like Dominicans at matins
or mothers in mourning,
stark against the sky's blue
and the lime of evergreen.

In the WMA there is no limit
during open crow season.
Still, they gather
in those leafless trees
exposed to the world
and all it can fire at them.

The stolid dread that rests
in those bare branches
must surely be something like
the fear that nests
in the brittle bones
that are our bodies,
if memory serves me well.

Elegy for a Lover Who Is Not Dead

The way you stand there
sleepless at the window
with the curtain pulled partly back
and even more the way
summer moonlight illumines your body

puts me in mind
of all the nights
we slept outside
under every phase
of that moon

and of how we watched
with distant curiosity
its body consumed
week by week
by a dark insatiable sky

In the end
what will take the place of love
if not this moon
and its prescient power
over the ebb and flow of desire?

Is it now some disarming dream
of moons that keeps you awake
or too much tomorrow
or thoughts of London
where you will sleep tonight?

Come back to bed, my love
I will wake you later
with tea and an orange
sliced the way you like
in quarters like the phases of our life

or would you prefer
a cool slice
of ripe melon
thin like the moon's body
once a month?

Correspondences

Man passes there through forests of symbols
Which look at him with understanding eyes.
—Charles Baudelaire

Sometimes out walking
we happen upon
things that matter

in winter for instance
that bare branches
become our brittle bones

in summer
thawed rivers arteries
that channel the blood

in fall
that leaves turn the color
of repentance

in spring
the mountain ablaze with fireweed
a full-length glass to mirror the soul

in the west
that the sun is a fire to signal
the beauty of our own decline

and beyond what the eye can see
a frontier approaching
fierce infinity

In the end what matters
is that we are the world's
and the world ours to keep

not like fireflies caught
and kept in a jar

but the image of us
and all we are

Montgomery Street

A poem for 8 voices

You can find them in antique shops
and sometimes flea markets
boxes of old postcards

you buy for a buck
or 20 for fifteen
with color photos

sometimes faded
and sometimes not
and in the blank space

on the other side
a note from
unknown travelers.

Here's one I found
one day in Ft. Worth
with a postmark of 1904:

Dear Folks:

Having a grand time
in old St. Lou.
Train ride here was a thrill.
You wouldn't believe
the things we've seen
at the World's Fair.

Love,

Dotty and Harold

And here's another
sent from Ruby Falls
I picked up in Pittsburgh:

Hello Sis:

We must have counted
100 signs that say
"See Rock City"
before we got here.
Sure is beautiful.
And much cooler
than Savannah.

See you soon,

Your big brother

And this one I love
with a lighthouse
on the Gulf of Mexico:

Dear Papa & Mama:

Walter and I made the drive
to Biloxi just fine.
We are so happy.
Thank you for
my beautiful wedding.

With all my love,

Mildred

Believe it or not
this one I bought
in Bainbridge
has a photo
of a street
and a row of houses

where I once lived
but is dated
50 years before.
See the blank
on the other side
and the note:

> *Dear Phyllis:*
>
> *I'm enjoying my visit*
> *with Aunt Helen*
> *Uncle Charles*
> *and Cousin Edgar*
> *very much.*
> *They all send*
> *their love and say*
> *you better come next time.*
>
> *Fondly,*
>
> *Edna*

I wanted to find
a magical card
and write in the blank:

Dear Edna:

So sorry I missed your visit.
I will look in on Helen
Charles and Edgar
or would be happy to
if I could find them in time.
Please come visit again
if you can.
I'd like to meet
Phyllis too.

What I found instead
was a poem written
in that house in Alabama

on Montgomery Street
waiting for autumn to arrive
the long summer Elvis died

with notes about
an old lover who died
giving birth

and a high school friend
who died too
but in a plane crash

and of falling in love
with the woman
who became an ex-wife.

I wanted to find a card
and send a note
back in time

to the man who wrote it
but the blank space
on the remembering

side of regret
was already full
so I continued reading

his notes to me
in the poem written then
from his reprobate heart:

> *One day they will*
> *tear down this house*
> *and all the houses*
> *where I've passed time*
>
> *and all the roads*
> *leading to them*
> *will lead nowhere*
> *and all that's left*
>
> *will be the space I've kept*
> *open and silent*
> *and the place of the mind*
> *that turns at the sound*

of a name
will go still
for silence has no need
for names

You can buy cards
like that for a buck
or 20 for fifteen

from boxes in dusty shops
and ragged flea markets
of the soul.

Crossing at Carthage

At Carthage following the flood
the boatman kills his motor
some thirty feet from shore
and we glide the final distance
to the dock for better fishing

On the river's far bank
a cottonfield gone to seed
among bramble and wild berries
black as the snakes
that rule the ground

And on this side
to which we have crossed
a canebrake thick with bamboo
mimosa and memories
of a place old as home

These banks were once
encampments of opposing armies
the boatman says
whose bodies bloated the water
and whose blood turned it red

As if the river were not a god
I imagined in turn *but a lamb*
sacrificed on the altar
of the sword to settle
a question of human freedom

Bowline in hand I leap forward
unmoored for a moment
to either land or water
but borne by better angels
until the gravity of my own

civil war of contradictions
brings me back down
to the defensible high ground
and the vulnerable valley
whose flank is unprotected

from sorties of infidelity
and doubt, jealousy and rage
promises made and pledges forgotten
and questions unanswered in the battle
between love and disdain

From this side to which we have crossed
we cast hope into our shadow selves
for channel cats and river bass
at Carthage after the flood
where fishing is better the boatman says

Killer Elite

You may stalk me down
a deserted street

choke me by the collar
against a brick wall and

drive a cold blade into my chest
I will donate my heart

as token of our chance meeting
even if its beat makes you live

with remembrance
of the cruel gesture

Bending the Bow

If the truth be told
every one of us believes
the man will return
one day
but none dares speak it
or his name.

Until then we hope and pretend
he has met the fate
that awaits all men—
dead at the hands of an angry god
or vengeful Trojan
swallowed whole by a sea
insatiable for human souls
or picked piecemeal from the field
by fattened crows—
and prefer our right
to the man's bed and wife
his wine and meat
if not his guile
his olive groves
his flocks of rams and ewes
on the grassy hills looking out to Kefalonia
to the fatherless boy prince
and to his crown.

If truth be known
the straight-backed woman

would have picked one of us
long ago to quiet the gossip
and return her island to order
had any one of us been worthy.

Truth is not every man
can be a warrior and king
husband and father
sailor and son.
Not every man can be a hero.
Not every man can win
a woman's heart.

And now this ragged old beggar
extends a challenge.
I put down my cup
and push my way
to the front of the pack.
The woman with hair
like a raven and eyes
deep like pools of wine
has handed him an ancient bow
from a locked room.
His eyes meet mine
with confident gaze.

String it and she is yours forever
he speaks in the voice of a prophet
her house forever
and all her land
and treasure forever—
but first take this bow
and bend it
if you can.

Jacob's Ladder

I am not he
the one to whom
a birthright was ceded
for a bowl of lentil stew

the favored one
whose dreams cast
angels commercing
between heaven and earth

climbing and descending
rungs of his celestial ladder

I am not he
I am the hairy
ruddy-faced twin
of the fields and bow

here heaven visits
not as angels
but indifferent
drops of rain

to settle the dust
if only for a time

I am not he
of the dream ladder
my means of ascent
are set firm in dust

and rise high enough
only to patch
holes in the roof
when I dream I feel

the son of a bitch's clutch
on my heel

pulling me back to earth
always pulling me back

Blue Umbrella

the one in the halltree rack
beside the entry door
one rib bent
another one cracked

a pole of whalebone
etched at the grip
and a canopy faded
but once the blue

of Bermuda waves
on the windward side
or perhaps nearing more
the hue of delphiniums

blooming wild
among Kansas sage—

in its transient stand
it is what remains

of the drizzly night
in Richmond and the
long walk to the bus ride home
of the downpour in Portland

while waiting for the boat
to Boothbay Harbor
of the storm forecast in
Phoenix that never fell

it is shade against forgetting
it is shelter from all loss
beside the door to coming
and to taking leave

Inheritance

It leans in the shade
against the white frame garage
a bike once red now rusted
through three layers of siblings
so much so it no longer has
a name of its own

But it is a Coke at Cashio's store
blackberries black snakes
and near-forgotten black graves
at Little Misery
a one-plank bridge to cross
in Thibodeaux Woods

It is the wind in your face
when you coast hands free
towards home
as dark settles in
Or is that the future
you feel rushing

headlong towards you
bringing with it
every woman
you will ever love
and all those
you will never find?

The Shape of Things

Water wearing the earth
Is the shape of the earth.
—Wendell Berry

So it is with remembering

Memory wearing the heart
is the shape of the heart

the river that carves the canyons
and smooths the stones

waters the wasteland
and unfenced patches of pasture

wettens and wakes snakes that uncoil
and thrust like the river itself

descends from mountain pools
or surfaces from deep springs

acquiescent to gravity
or the land's internal pressure

the Big Muddy
that marks the boundary

between the Louisiana of desire
and the Mississippi of regret

the Missouri that reaches
the great divide

between living
and its rumored witness

the Colorado diverted
by the dam of denial

All life it seems
is a matter of mapping

contour and relief
sadness and faith

what is done
and what remains

So it is with remembering

The Speed of Believing

What we see happens faster
than what we hear
traveling as it does
at the speed of sight,
and sound is swifter in turn
than what we at last believe,
like lightning and thunder
for instance,
or closer to mind

the way smoke as we near
a flame across the field
ascends before we hear
crackling of the logs
or have the thought
that smoke rising
is the soul of fire
seeking a world less hot
or believe that such a world exists.

What we deny
happens fastest of all
like the news
that you were gone,
my prodigal brother,
found alone and broke
dead from an imperfect heart
broken further by betrayals
and addiction to self-doubt.

When the furnace burned
your body to ash
I wondered
if the wisps of smoke
rising from the oven flue
were the ghosts of your flame
seeking some other world
but could not be sure
since believing is so slow.

Music from Another Room

At this moment
the music of Massenet
is being played
in an apartment
down the hall

an obscure piece
I recognize
from a woman
who taught piano
in Antwerp
in a cramped room
on *den Boulevard*
with space for only
the grand instrument
and two chairs

and in the evenings
took walks
with other women
down to the river
to watch the sun set
on the Scheldt
and the bluestone quays
and the ships sailing in

and then drank wine
late into the night
in the Bocadero

and talked with
those women
and with sailors
from the ships
about their cargos
and diamonds

and sometimes took
a sailor home
and made love
in a bedroom
next to the
cramped music room

and in the morning
after her lover
had left
played piano
until it was time
to receive students

who could hear
Massenet's sole concerto
as they walked
down the hall
to her apartment

Blue Cardigan

It hangs in the closet
out of season
and out of style
a well-worn sweater
the blue as one might remember
the light between
twilight and dark
the night of his passing

in that space between
he did his best dying

and in the space that remains
what was left that matters—
besides some odd ties
and faded photographs—
is the loose-fitting form
of a father
in the wardrobe between
summer clothes and the fall

Snow Falling on Stones

I.

the stillness of winter:
        snow covers the path

the poet sits by the crackle
        of logs he had cut

turning to heat and light
        the only other sounds

the whisper of a page turning
        and a thought turning

like snow falling on stones
        in the stillness of winter

II.

the first green of spring
was not in the garden
or along the path

but in the promise of daffodil
and wild iris at river's edge

unlike the daffodil and iris
the poet knows his days
trace an arc not a circle

but still the promise of daffodil
and wild iris at river's edge

III.

the poet walked
the path to the river

he heard a morning sound

the last fall goose signal
its rise through fog

lifting from the water

in his walk
the poet came to know

what the river knows

IV.

thunder rolled
down the mountain

in the sky-darkened garden
the poet silently counted

the breaths between
thunder and lightning

with each breath
the poet smelled

the coming storm
in the slight tremor

of pine branches
and amaryllis

the first drops fell
the poet felt them

one by one on his head
face and shoulders

the poet silently counted
the breaths between drops

with each breath
the poet smelled

the coming days between
summer & September

with each breath
the poet smelled
the breath of God

V.

the poet had
but one thought all day:

tears of an old lover
upon parting

and the sweet smell
of lilacs in the rain

the poet carried
that thought all day:

a ripe pear
brown-speckled yellow

and newly soft
to his touch

at day's end the poet
sliced the pear

and fed on its
sweet soft sadness

VI.

each poem was a stone
skipped across the face
of the River Wye

one day the poet learned
what causes ripples
must also sink

VII.

in the poem
was a dream of deer
feeding near the river

and the heart of deer
was itself a poem
wanting to be spoken

The Theory of Everything

If we do discover a theory of everything . . .
it would be the ultimate triumph of human reason—
for then we would truly know the mind of God.
—Stephen Hawking

A partial truth
is not a lie
or a single jigsaw
piece a falsehood

perhaps it's just the way
Truth likes to play
coy at cards
and puzzles

the way for instance
winter's first snow
stretches a blank canvas
across the landscape

of imagination
and lets experience
supply the paints
and memory the brushes

or the way sunlight
lengthens only
by degrees in spring
until the solstice comes

Early one evening
as Cambridge students strolled
from dormitories to dining halls
and crews rowed the Cam

it dawned on the esteemed
physicist that perhaps
we cannot in the end
know the mind of God

except to know
that the mind of God
is never made up
of finalities

I like to think it happened
during a game of cards
with Cambridge colleagues
and Newton's ghost

when the first hand dealt
could not be gambled
and the ace and king
came only later

or maybe he saw Truth
as the real striptease act
bumping and grinding
down to its birthmark

but not all at once
not just yet
leaving something for a time
to the imagination

Birding in the Bend

Some scan the tops of trees
with high-powered binoculars

others train sights
on single branches or nests

and some seek it
at pond's edge

quiet at the margins
among cattails and reeds:

a vision beatific of birds
in the bend of the Arkansas

kingbird and teal
needle-billed phalarope

canvasback and snow goose
rock pigeon and plover

With Bushnells or Athlons in hand
we glimpse more sharply

meadowlarks and wood thrush
herons and grackles

but only seeing closes the space
between us and birds

no more than it does
the distance to love

or God or any other thing
that bends perches or flies

The Light from Dying Stars

In Arkansas
the water in thermal baths
began as rain
or melted snow
that found its way
into mountain fissures
and trickled down
for eight thousand years
before reaching hot springs

On earth
the light from stars
began as burning spheres
of hydrogen and helium
that found its way
through the atmosphere
and trickled down
trillions of miles
before reaching our eyes

Neil deGrasse Tyson speculates
that Vega, Arcturus or Sirius
could have burned themselves out
before they light our sky
and that their flame
is only a memory—
only time could tell
he says if we had
worlds enough and time

Nietzsche speculated also
that God is dead
as if God
were a sphere of gas
that flamed out in time
and is only distant memory
perhaps time will tell
but we look
for the light anyway

Gate 23

Weather delay at Hartsfield
random grey day between
somewhere and home

paperback in hand
to pass the time
notebook and pen
for passing thoughts

final calls for boarding overhead
parts of conversations overheard
Cinnabon smells
a sailor stretched out
and snoring
two seats over
a trio of nuns
in traditional habit
(they never travel alone)
a family of four
returning from Disney
(the mouse ears are proof)
in the concourse the
beep of the courtesy tram
and the flow of entranced passengers
like fish in a river
swimming upstream or down

Weather has cleared
random grey day brightens
between somewhere and home

the procession of pilgrims
boarding passes ready
one more counter to clear
in this coincidental life

If My Voice

If my voice could be an instrument
it could be a trumpet triumphant
and true, maybe mellow like Miles
when he found his groove
in *Kind of Blue.*

If my voice could be an instrument
it could be a saxophone cooking
like Coleman who gave it a home,
or Coltrane in his stride on *A Love Supreme*
blowing kisses up to God.

If my voice could be an instrument
it could charm like a clarinet
the way an Indian charmer can
snakes out of a basket, or the way
Gershwin's "Summertime" is coaxed by Bechet.

If my voice could be an instrument
it could sit in on all-night jams
at The Spotted Cat once the joint closed down
holding back, giving back, and given the rein
taking the lead like a cat out on the town.

If my voice could be an instrument
it wouldn't swing or bop like Bassie,
but make the girls all go crazy
and want to dance slow and close
the way only true love does.

If my voice could be an instrument
let it be an instrument of peace
a jazz St. Francis beatific
making lovers out of fighters
turning mourners into believers

if my voice could be an instrument.

Lacunae

This is not another poem
about locust infestations
or viruses that captivate earth.
Instead it offers words
to fill the hollow spaces
between us when
there is no earthquake in Haiti
or tsunami in Japan
no trade towers crumbling
or meteor streaking
towards our home

words to plaster the cracks

in history when we forget
or God fails to remind us
that the poor are
with us always
and of the silent sadnesses
of those among us
who daily clutch loneliness
like a hard jewel
polished smooth by
the oily rag of longing
on slow news days

Vigilance

Be sure to pick the olive
before the breeze down
from the barren hills
fills the grove
with it sadness

Be sure to pick the fig
just as it turns
the shade of a deep bruise
before grey palomas
return to peck at the pain

But do not rush to gather
the one ragged from the field
or dusty from the boat
whose Catalan
is not the king's

Spare that one a while
from the brusque harvest
in your bushel basket of bars

Falling Asleep Before Dark

Walk as children of the light.
—Ephesians 5:8

Falling asleep before dark
as the evening news begins
into a place beyond dream
another world where sleep
is for sleep and not escape

In that world
a hard rain falls
on the just and unjust alike

solders strip off
waterlogged fatigues
until they are cold and wet
as the day they were born
and like the babies
they once were
cannot speak yet
the word for *hate*
in any language
and naked as newborns
can no longer tell
friend from foe

In that world too
the rain turns to snow
and then to leaves of paper
falling from military planes
like manna in the desert
and reading:

Due to factory strike
We have no bombs.
Go home to your mothers.
War is canceled today.

In that world
the only clamor and din
is the psalm
of dew forming
on rusted tanks
and on the grass of graves
rooted in the hearts
of beautiful young corpses

And in that world
the dew sings
just before the day
succumbs to total darkness
and the evening news
concludes:
Blessed are the peacemakers
they shall be called
children of God

What I Meant to Say

It holds more
than I wish to speak

that dream of waking
in a forest of petrified trees
and fog

and in the highest branch
of the tallest tree
a screech owl with apricot eyes

only to say
that waking

was like the end
of love as we knew it
or wished it to be

and trees the hardest thing
that ever seemed real—

now that it's
late in winter years later

what I meant to say
but did not know it
at the time was that

screeching apricots in dense air
were the lesser gods
between evil and loneliness

Second Comings

And without are dogs and sorcerers
—Revelation 22:15

In childhood the dream
was the same
those thunderous nights

in summer
in the bottom bunk
of the bedroom
in Baton Rouge:

the coming again
of Christ
both awaited and feared

on rolling clouds
at once dark and luminous
as if painted
by Caravaggio or the Greek

and the waking
the same as well—
not to howling

of dogs in the dark
at thunder's holy terror
or to tricked flashes
of lightning—

but to a quaking
border collie bounding
onto the bed

and startling the boy
into its own fright
from whatever apocalyptic dreams
dogs have on dreadful nights

and forcing one
young as me
to embrace fear

and to know it
as something
luminous and dark
furry and wet

but to know fear now
alone in a sudden midnight storm
on the open Kansas plains

is to know that God will not return
in dreams—we must look for God
instead in the globe of quivering light
flickering all around like a dying bulb

or in the single doe
that emerged this morning
from scattered pieces of calm

stepping cautiously back into the world
along the gravel road then darting
disappearing into tall prairie grass
high as the mane on a prize pony

About the Author

A native of Baton Rouge, Michael Blanchard now lives in the Cadron Valley of Central Arkansas, where he is an adjunct professor of literature at the University of Central Arkansas and editor of *SLANT,* UCA's international journal of contemporary poetry. He has also taught at Troy State University (where he was presented the Ingalls Award for Excellence in Classroom Teaching), North Carolina State University, and the University of Louisiana.

For 20 years, he was also an advocate for compassionate care of the sick and dying through his work with hospice organizations in Louisiana and North Carolina. Previous publications include four other books of poetry, the most recent of which is *The Pearl Diver's Daughter & Other Poems* (2023). His poems can also be found in *Alabama Literary Review, Quarry, Voyeur, Cave Region Review, Bayou Magazine, MockingHeart Review, Stone Poetry Quarterly,* and *Streetlight Magazine,* among others.

www.ingramcontent.com/pod-product-compliance
Lightning Source LLC
LaVergne TN
LVHW090616110826
845146LV00001B/417
9798901468074